Scripturally Structured

"A Guide To Business Success"

According To God's Word

Jennifer S. Simmons

JENNIFER S. SIMMONS

Copyright © 2017 Jennifer S. Simmons

All rights reserved.

ISBN: 1537072072

ISBN-13: 978-1537072074

DEDICATION

I dedicate this book to the sacredness of true love, friendship, sisterhood and brotherhood. Your impression on my life is permanent. The bond we have is unbreakable!

CONTENTS

Acknowledgments

1	Fear	1
2	Planning for Success	6
3	Failure	12
4	Budgeting	17
5	Moving in Silence	24
6	Launching a Business	29
7	Networking	36
8	Time Management	41
9	Operations	45
10	Conclusion	57

ACKNOWLEDGMENTS

To my parents Alfred and Lillie Simmons. Dad, your gardening skills taught me the importance of watching the seeds that you planted grow through preparation, care and maintenance. The reward came at the time of harvest. This book is my time of harvest. Mom, I watched you work while you and dad raised seven children. Not only did you work, but you went to college and managed to start your own successful business in floral design. Your ambition and work ethic contributed to the adult I became.

To my siblings Clay, Clayetta, Alberta, Melissa, Brian and Jaquetta while we are all different, we are all family and I couldn't be me without you being you. Thank you for loving me like you do.

To my nieces and nephews Tracena, Alfreda, DeEtta, Lashie, Ashanti, Jayvon, Brian Jr, Belinda, Vincent, Victor, Teijuan, Elijah, Christian, AJ, Julian and Monte I am especially doing this for you. Whatever you want to achieve in life, I am here to make certain you do so. Your future will be great because God has already promised this to all of us.

We are the Simmonses!

CHAPTER ONE

Fear

"But whoever listens to me will live in safety and be at ease; without fear of harm."
- Proverbs 1:33

If you've ever dreamed of launching your own business the time is now! What are you waiting for? God's promises of prosperity, success and happiness may come with a little hard work, but they are obtainable. He mentions in the referenced scripture that if we listen to His instructions, He can assure our safety. I'm certain there are more questions than answers when you embark on this journey. You may find yourself fearing the uncertainties of starting a business such as finances, other people's opinions, and unworthiness. Being scripturally structured in your business means that you believe God secures us. This means He gives us everything we need to be fully equipped for the task at hand. There are a few key elements that I want to share with you to help you feel even more secure and fearless as a new business owner. The formula to conquer fear is **Will + Might + Faith = Fearlessness**.

- **Will** - Your will takes effect at the very moment you decide on and initiate the action of becoming an entrepreneur.

- **Might** - Might is the power to move forward with the decision and take the necessary steps to achieving your goals.

- **Faith** - Faith is believing that you will accomplish everything you set out to do successfully.

The road to being completely fearless can be a long journey for some. It certainly depends on your level of faith, but also on your current circumstances and your confidence level. Confidence is going to be a key factor throughout the life of your business. Confidence is all about believing in yourself and/or your abilities. If you don't believe in yourself or your product, how do you expect someone else to? If you truly believe in God's promises you will not consider your financial circumstances a hindrance.

Taking a look at some other reasons one may be fearful in presenting themselves as a business owner, I reflect on my own journey. I often thought about how others would receive me or my products/services. I feared people would think I wasn't qualified or worthy of the gifts God gave me. I also thought about my financial situation; all I had was an idea with no start-up capital to back me up.

My Power Boost!

I asked myself, "What natural gifts has God given me?" He has given me things that I didn't learn, yet have the ability to do. So, my power boost came from knowing that nobody could do these things better than me because God gave them to me. That was enough to push me to really do this. There will always be critics; either they like it or they don't, either they support or they won't. Everything is parallel and has opposites. Which parallel will I put myself in? Which parallel will you put yourself in? Once you move forward, fear can no longer exist. This doesn't mean that you won't have anxiety, but you cannot take fear with you on your journey.

Have you ever seen a deer freeze when faced with the headlights of a vehicle as it approaches? Imagine yourself being that deer, afraid to take a chance on your ideas. This is the same crippling feeling that takes over our bodies when we are faced with the challenge of sharing or presenting our project. The fear takes control of your mind, body and soul; clouding our judgment and stopping progress. Fear will cause you to go left when it makes sense to go right, and you cannot make sound business decisions with clouded judgment.

Critics may have all of the ideas, but not the 3 elements: will, might, and faith. One day I thought, "Why do I allow other people's opinions to matter?" It was at that moment that I started conquering fear and counting my blessings.

In 2 Timothy 1:7, we are reminded that God gave us a spirit that is not timid; He gave us power and self-discipline. So, discipline yourself to not act on your fears but recognize and utilize the power that is already inside of you. When you find yourself questioning this refer to Joshua 1:9, "Have I not commanded you? Be strong and courageous do not be afraid; do not be discouraged, for the LORD your God will be with you wherever you go."

"Don't let fear stop you from being great!"

Pastor Shannon McRae

Life Transformation Ministries

Columbia, SC

CHAPTER TWO

Planning For Success

Commit thy works unto the Lord, and thy thoughts shall be established."
-Proverbs 16:3

If you believe it, you can achieve it - this phrase may seem like a cliché, but it is true. Have you ever heard of speaking life into the atmosphere?

I was that little girl who always had a dream of being in charge of something. In elementary school, being in charge meant taking names of classmates who misbehaved when the teacher stepped out of the room or being responsible for feeding the class pet. In middle school, it meant being the head of student council and reporting students without a hall pass to the principal, being president of the seventh grade earth club or the teacher's assistant grading papers during my recess period. I found pleasure in knowing for those moments I was the boss of that job, and I took great pride in the work I was doing. All along I was being prepped for my role in life today, the role of an entrepreneur.

Sometimes the human eye can't see beyond the natural abilities we possess. Never would I have imagined what or who I was destined to be. God placed me in those situations to mold me for my future. There may be people in your life telling you it can't be done, but they aren't familiar with God's plan for you. All your life God has placed you in situations to prepare you for your future as an entrepreneur. Take a few minutes to think back and reflect on your life experiences or the people whose paths you've crossed. All of that was purposely, scripturally structured in order for you to become your future self. Right now it doesn't matter your education or skill level. If you have the desire, let's break down your steps to becoming scripturally structured in your business initiative.

If you have the skill, but lack the knowledge there is always room for intellectual growth. If you are looking to do something you have absolutely no experience in; your key ingredient is FAITH. No matter which category you may find yourself in, the same path is required.

I found myself in the category of having the skill with no direction; knowing there was a gift inside of me that I was freely giving away to people. I had to realize that my time mattered and my gifts and talents held value.

This may not be your story, however, James 1:5 says, "If any of you lacks wisdom, let him ask God, who gives generously to all without reproach, and it will be given him." It's really that simple, ask and you shall receive.

After asking, God tells us in the reference scripture that if we commit our works unto the Lord, our thoughts shall be established.

Let's spend some time talking about your overall business template. Your very first steps will consist of developing a detailed business plan that will be the guide to your business practices. This plan simply allows you to set measurable goals for your business that will determine your overall success over a period of time. Here are a few pertinent components of a business plan:

Executive Summary

Use this introduction to your business plan to really paint the picture for potential investors. Readers will be more likely or willing to invest in your endeavor if your summary is descriptive and clearly paints the picture what types of services or products your business will offer. Remember it is just a summary so keep it concise, goal-oriented and purposeful.

Business Structure

The foundation of your business should be described in your mission statement. Whether you are a sole proprietor in business for yourself, or working to build a larger corporation, you cannot skip this step in the process. This portion of your business plan should be very specific as to what types of services or products you will offer, unique features of your offerings and the location of your facility.

SWOT Analysis

A swot analysis is where you measure the strengths, weaknesses, opportunities and threats of your business. Strengths would include how you feel you measure up against your competitors and why you feel you do or don't have a competitive advantage. When looking at your weaknesses be honest with yourself. If you don't have the financial resources needed to effectively run your business you can clearly state that in this category. Opportunities are where you have the chance to propose new potential for your business. Threats are just that; anything you feel would be a threat to your business. By conducting an honest swot analysis you are preparing yourself for the fight in working to your great earning potential.

Budget

When creating a budget, you are setting the amount you will need to start and maintain your business. My suggestion is to develop an expense budget for each quarter of the year. This will be further explained in Chapter 4.

"Vision only hands you the lenses to search for what you need to be successful, but strategy comes through perseverance and dedication to follow through with what you see."

Nefateri Smalls

Healing Hurts

Ridgeville, SC

CHAPTER THREE

Dealing with Failures

"Like a dog that returns to its vomit, a fool does the same foolish things again and again."
- Proverbs 26:11

Quite the vivid scripture to reference for failure, but oh so true. Believe me when I say that I lived failure throughout the process of writing this book. I experienced set backs, feelings of doubt and insignificance and all of the emotions associated with failure. It taught me to push a little harder, dig a little deeper and find a level of strength that far outweighed any side effects of the failure itself. The good things about failing is that you learn from it. Many people would never believe if I; prior to earning a Bachelors of Arts in Management and prior to earning my Masters in Business Administration made several failed attempts at completing a college education. Honestly, I rarely completed anything that I started. I wanted to be a marine biologist, a chef, a photographer, nail technician, hairstylist...the list goes on. I was full of great ideas but had the hardest time executing them. I'm not ashamed to admit my biggest failure to all of you. In 1992 I repeated my sophomore year of high school. I am not proud of it; however it has shaped me into becoming who I am so I don't regret that it happened to me. The thing about failure that is the hardest to deal with is finding your own fault in the situation. We don't want to take ownership of the reason we failed at something. I had to take ownership in the role I played that caused me to fail and could not blame it on my friends, my teachers or my surroundings. It was up to me to be responsible for my own outcome. I shared off of that to help you understand when we fail it is important to accept the failure as a learning opportunity and move on.

Most of us find our lowest moments are the times when we've made an attempt at something and failed. It's the perception of it, whether you want to look at the glass half empty or half full. Failure isn't an end to a great idea or concept, it is really a new beginning. It allows that reflection time to review and analyze to determine where you can determine what worked well and what didn't work well. It should be a time of isolation and solitude for you. Not to hide from the consequences of the failure, but to recharge and think without the input or pressures of your peers.

For many throughout history failure has been a part of the process of success:

- **Thomas Edison**: Edison made 1,000 unsuccessful attempts at inventing the light bulb

- **Michael Jordan**: Jordan was cut from his high school basketball team twice

- **Harrison Ford**: In his first film, Ford was told by the movie execs that he simply didn't have what it takes to be a star

- **Oprah Winfrey**: Winfrey was fired from her job as a television reporter because she was "unfit for tv."

- **Sidney Poitier**: After his first audition, Poitier was told by the casting director, "Why don't you stop wasting people's time and go out and become a dishwasher or something?

Let me pose this questions; what if they stopped? What if after being let down, belittled and disappointed they never tried again? We would not have electricity as we know today, we would have never experienced the famous the moments Michael Jordan gave us in the dunk contest, I would not have had one of my favorite movies, "Air Force One" to enjoy with the hero Harrison Ford, Oprah would not have been the great example and role model she is for us and without Sidney Poitier the path would not have been paved for others to follow in his footsteps.

Your success is a must. God doesn't bless us for us; he gives us gifts and abilities to glorify him so that others can be led to him and so that we can be a blessing of encouragement to others. We all have someone who sees us as someone they look up to. Whether it be a child or an envying adult; somehow, our presence and our contributions create a balance in the atmosphere of the world. We cannot allow failure to cripple us. Instead, let failure be your guide.

> *"Don't let other people's opinions of you make you feel like a failure before you even try."*

Pastor Lillie Simmons

Mighty Warriors For Christ

Summerville, SC

CHAPTER FOUR

Budgeting

"The rich man's wealth is his strong city: the destruction of the poor is their poverty."
- Proverbs 10:15

"The rich rule over the poor and the borrower is slave to the lender."
- Proverbs 22:7

Remember in grade school when they told you that you would use mathematics every day for the rest of your life? They were telling the truth. If you missed a few principles along the way, I highly recommend that you take an online course in accounting. I also suggest that you study the scriptures that are presented to you in this chapter as a guide to your money handling and your way of thinking, especially if you have a business partner.

Some call money the root of all evil, others call it the trump card that allows you to exert power. Yes, it does give you certain leverage in life; however, having an abundance of it does not make you superior at all. Just like anything else, it has a life span and there is a beginning and an ending to how much and how long you will have it without proper budgeting. Whatever you do, don't let the fact that you may not have any money available at this moment discourage your from your plans of becoming an entrepreneur or continuing your business if you fall on hard times. When we think about money, instantly there are two categories of people; those who have a lot of it and those who have little or none. The ownership of such possessions and status that comes with it gives individuals a certain level of being; simply stating it messes with your level of confidence. A rich man knows his place in society and they are well received by most. This in turn causes them to have a level of happiness that is wholly revolved around their possessions. It's the people who have less that have a hard time finding where they fit into society; yet they are happy with the simpler things life has to offer, like family or friends. Money, just like in a marriage, friendship or relationship with family members, can be divisive if there aren't clear discussions and boundaries in how it will be spent and saved. Discussing how money should be saved may be a new concept for you. It is certainly logical when spending money but not a norm to talk about saving it. Saving money is going to become the most beneficial quality you possess. Too often we see people who at some point had it "good" in our eyes. They had the best house, the best car, the best clothes, etc., but their bank account was a zero or even worse, in the negative. Not exactly someone you want to idolize when it comes to budgeting. So, how on earth do you save money when you don't see where you can spare it? I'll take this on by asking you a series of questions:

1. How often do you pick up a penny off of the ground when you see one?

2. How often do you stop by a fast food restaurant a week?

3. Do you buy groceries for the month or do you buy packages for the day?

4. Do you take your lunch to work or do you buy lunch?

5. Do you swipe a debit card for every transaction or do you get enough cash to last you until your next paycheck?

I just wanted to give you a few questions for you to really think about where your dollars are going. Chances are if your answers reflected your expenditures are excessive, you are finding yourself with a zero or negative balance before your next paycheck; and you should consider a change in how you manage your funds. The way you handle your personal finances is a hint of how you will also handle your business finances. This path does not lead to a road of success. When you look at what you are spending, it's quite possible that you could fund your own business without help from others. Let's take a look at the latter of Proverbs 22:7 "The borrower is slave to the lender". Certainly, if you find yourself having to borrow funds to start your business there is nothing wrong with this, in my opinion. You only become slave to the lender if you borrow above the means in which you have to pay them back. With the right planning you should be able to estimate your earnings and your ability to pay the loan back before accruing interest (same as cash). At this point you should have a dollar amount in mind that you would like to have to start your business with. I highly recommend you start with enough operating capital (cash on hand) to take you through at least 2 quarters (6 months). Don't be so hasty to start if your finances aren't in place, pace yourself. You may also consider investors, business partners or grant-funders.

Every successful business (with success being defined by measuring your goals) should have a budget. In this budget start with two main factors your assets and your liabilities. Assets would be items such as your available cash on hand and liabilities would include your expenses. In my experience it is wise to calculate your expenses first, considering you may be a start-up business with no funds available. Leave no stone unturned when developing this budget. Even budget for the unexpected, for example, if a machine breaks or there is a natural disaster and you are unable to work. Also, budget for staff or maybe an assistant if you are starting out small. Think about your marketing, operations costs, rent, utilities, and supplies. My point - in calculating your expenses and your current assets you should also consider your earnings, this will measure your ability to operate your business and earn revenue.

Also remember, when budgeting, consider your own value. What are you worth? What will you charge for your products or services? These are important questions that will aid you in your earnings estimates. It is easy to price a product and put a value to that. Don't allow your time to be wasted if you are offering a service. Place a value on YOU. People will respect you and what you have to offer more if it is weighted with a price. If you offer a free service some may see it as you not valuing what you have to offer; and let's face it you get what you pay for. I'd rather pay for a great service than receive a free service that has no value or benefit to me. If you need help with pricing do a market analysis to find out what other people in the same field are charging for their products and services. Fit yourself in the middle; high enough to turn a profit, but low enough to gain and retain customers of your competitors.

In all, budgeting in addition to planning is

extremely important to the future of your business. Think highly enough of yourself and your business to budget every aspect of spending and saving; and poverty will not be your ruin. It won't even be in your vocabulary.

"One's mind and body must be one with God in order to obtain incredible wealth."

Pastor Torrest Richardson

Kingdom Life International

Moncks Corner, SC

CHAPTER FIVE

Moving In Silence

"The prudent keep their knowledge to themselves, but a fool's heart blurts out folly." (NIV)
- Proverbs 12:23

'm certain you are anxious to share your new business idea with your friends and family. While sharing this news may bring you great joy; often times it also brings unwanted advice and opinions.

At this point, you should have developed a stronger sense of faith and fear should no longer be an issue. Please know that other's opinions tend to taint or water down the effectiveness of your gift, service or product. You must understand that the opinions of others may not be coming from a celebratory standpoint, but of jealousy and envy for "a fool's heart blurts out folly." People will support you until you reach a level of success that they feel like you don't deserve. This is why moving in silence is extremely important. So, when we talk about a person being prudent, a prudent person gives great thought to their future. They are concerned with outcomes and how their outcomes will affect others. Most importantly, they walk on the side of caution and discreetly nurture what they are about to birth. Others' opinions of you and your business usually come from their level of faith, not your level of faith.

So, why can't you tell your friends and family about your new business? Nobody will care about your business more than you, therefore you have to protect it because it is your brainchild; from the loins of your brain. A lesson my mom taught me was to always be smarter than the next man, woman, boy or girl. At the moment that you share your business with someone, the questions are asked, "Can I get a freebie?", "Can I get a hook-up?", or "Can I get a discount?" You will put your all into your work and you will give a great service, but your return on investment will be zero.

Naturally, you may want to seek advice from a veteran in your field. Here is what I've found is that a veteran, who may have more resources and a larger network, may take your great idea and run with it. My advice to you, if you feel the need to speak to someone in that field, make sure you can trust them and have your idea patented. By doing this, you have protected your creation. Sharing your news prematurely puts you in danger of gaining superficial support, you know, the kind of support that comes with conditions. Your friends and family are usually the biggest offenders. They will sometimes paint the picture that you are somehow benefiting from their support, but actually they are the ones benefitting the most. Again I say, move in silence! During this phase of your start-up, the last thing you'll need is disappointments because they will set you back. An added benefit of moving in silence is if for some reason things don't go as planned, you can make the necessary adjustments. And, if things don't work out, you can fail in silence.

Remember what you present to people will be the first impressions of you or your business. Operating in silence allows you the opportunity to make sure that your product or service has been prepared and tested. So, when you store up knowledge, you are doing your necessary research and learning your trade first hand and not by the mouths of others. This now makes you an expert in your trade or field.

One thing to remember, your favor is your favor! This means the blessings that are in store for you belong to you, and no one else is entitled to reap your benefits. Moving in silence also allows you to protect that favor, your mind and your spirit. Sharing your plans with people tend to have the effect of lowering your confidence; therefore hindering your process. Remember when Noah was working on building an arc. What did people say about him? They said he was crazy, he was a fool, etc. What if Noah had allowed what people said about him to hinder his work? Where would we be? Remember, there is a certain law of nature that is called cause and effect. Everything we do today will affect our tomorrow or someone else's tomorrow. If your confidence level is down, you won't be able to perform at your best. You'll operate under a different set of rules, being you are trying to prove yourself to people in a way that has a negative effect on you. Let the proof of your worth come from your work, the completed project. Show them what you're capable of; then you won't waste precious moments trying to verbally tell them. Let people stand in awe and wonder about what you were able to do with God's help.

"When God gives an assignment, it's better to walk in the spirit of obedience. Please keep in mind, the assignment was given to you, therefore it doesn't need to be validated by others."

Evangelist Senika Londa Walker

Trinity Holiness Church of Deliverance

Moncks Corner, SC

CHAPTER SIX

Presenting Your Business: Marketing & Networking

"Plans fail for lack of counsel, but with many advisers they succeed." (NIV)
- *Proverbs 15:22*

Marketing

Before moving forward let's define marketing. Marketing, as defined by the American Marketing

Association is the activity, set of institutions, and processes for creating, communicating, delivering, and exchanging offerings that have value for customers, clients, partners, and society at large.

Further, promotion is the act of encouraging others. Once your product or service has been tested and has measured up to being ready for the world to see, you have to consider how you will present it to people with a strategic marketing plan. Strategically launching and marketing your business may initially be perceived as a challenge. The biggest challenge is developing your plan so that you have a checklist to go by; executing your plan is the easy part. You first need a marketing budget to help spread the word about your new business. Each dollar should have a specific place to be allocated whether it is television, radio, newspaper or social media. You should also consider whether you want to only promote and bring awareness to your brand locally, regionally (across neighboring state lines), or nationally.

Brand Recognition Marketing

Branding is going to be very important to the life of your business. How you or your company is perceived is important to how others will rate your services; or even if they will consider your services. Some of the things people will look at when considering your brand is how much of an edge you have over your competitors. Your brand will either be the better brand or the lowest quality. The foundation of your brand is your logo. If your logo is distasteful chances are the results of your work may be also. Your website, packaging and promotional materials, all of which should include your logo, communicate your brand to the people. When someone thinks of your brand they should instantly be able to link your logo and/or a catchy jingle to you.

Social Media Marketing

Social media marketing is one of the best things that could ever happen to a small business with a small budget for marketing. Social media allows you to market directly to people you are already connected to. These are the first people you may look to for support of your business. It allows you to make posts daily for free; however, if you pay for advertising you can reach a broader audience. Another great thing is it allows you to select a target market (age group, sex, location) to market to. After creating and completing a marketing campaign, social media will provide you with actual data helping you to hone in your real market. This may be a good way to determine your real target audience prior to paying for higher priced advertising on radio and television.

Radio and Television Marketing

While radio is a great source for people to hear about your brand via a radio jingle commercial or even a radio interview; television gives that special touch of people being able to hear and see which helps one retain information about your brand. These will be great sources for you to utilize in spreading the news. Because radio and television may be more costly than other marketing options it is really important for you to research and know your demographic. Your demographic is going to be your potential customers. For example, if your brand is selling sneakers that is for the youth then you need to know the best time of day to air your commercial and what outlets have the ear or eye of the youth. It may be great for a television commercial during a cartoon that comes on after school hours. Knowing this information will help you not to waste your marketing dollars. When considering radio do not forget about internet radio stations who may reach a larger audience than your local stations.

Brand Enhancement

It is important to keep your product/good or services up to standard according to the needs of the consumer. Sometimes you have to re-invent or enhance your offerings to stay valid, retain your loyal customers and keep people interested; especially if the market is saturated with people offering the same things you are. Think about some of the brands you may be loyal to, for example, I love Oreo cookies. What Nabisco had to do to keep Oreos relevant after so many decades is enhance the product. They started with Oreo doublestuff, then a variety of filling flavors for the season, then the yellow cookie with chocolate center. All of these changes kept the consumer coming for more. Another example is Gain laundry detergent. How many different scents do they have? What new products did they develop over time to accompany their original detergent products? There are a variety of scents to choose from along with dryer sheets and other Gain-scented household cleaning products. I used those examples to show that no company is exempt from having to make changes to their brand to offset what their competitors are doing. Again, it helps your company stay valid and your customers stay loyal to you.

Launching

The right time to launch a business is going to depend on what you have to offer. By now you should have already completed a demographic survey of people in your company to find that there is a need for your service or product. Now you need to let them know that your goods or services are available to them. If you are selling products visual launches work best. This will be a time where you can display your items to possible investors and consumers. Investors will be more willing to partner with you if they can see an iron clad, durable product or your services are beneficial and will aid in strengthening the community. If you prefer to have a launch, compare it to a small wedding. You have to run a business after your launch. Don't put too much money into, but make it count. A launch is not necessary for you to be successful. By having a strong marketing presence and grassroots networking, you will be just fine in starting to work your business without a formal launch event.

Planning out your marketing strategy will allow you to seek counsel from the professionals. Remember, your friends, family and competitors can't help you in this area. While you are talking to radio and television sales professionals, logo designers, graphic designers and all those who specialize in marketing on a daily basis you should absorb every piece of knowledge they share with you.

"Marketing entails more than just spending money. It involves strategic planning, and knowing how and where to make the money that you spend to market yourself, work effectively for you."

Tony D

Christian Sounds Entertainment

CHAPTER SEVEN

Networking

"My son, do not let wisdom and understanding out of your sight, preserve sound judgment and discretion; they will be life for you, an ornament to grace your neck. Then you will go on your way in safety, and your foot will not stumble."
-Proverbs 3:21-23 (NIV)

Remember the age old saying, "Watch the company you keep?" One of the hardest lessons you can learn will be the result of being in the wrong place at the wrong time with the wrong people. It's a life lesson that applies to business as well. I'd like to get just a little bit spiritual for a moment. God gives us all innate gifts that we have naturally at birth, and he also gives spiritual gifts to those who accept Jesus as their personal savior. Whether innate or acquired later in life; the gift of discernment will be of most value to you in your networking process. Discernment allows you to be a good judge of character and gives you a level of spiritual direction given directly from God. With this gift you will know just by a feeling or a vibe that things in the atmosphere just aren't right. It's that little still voice that says walk away when you want to continue to move forward.

Networking, why is this important? One of the things that will be continuous throughout the life of your business is networking. Networking is going to bring you 40% of your business, word of mouth 40% and paid advertisements 20%. These are my own personal statistics in my experience of operating a business. You are going to come in contact with people who you should always, initially, see as a potential customer or business connection. I say, initially, because time will tell if their intentions or business practices match with yours. Referencing the above scripture; sound judgment is going to be an ornament to grace your neck. Bad judgment could be an ornament to strangle your neck.

Networking simply stated is sharing your information and services with a group of people who have an interest in what you are doing or vice versa. It's somewhat of an art when you have the attention of someone and there is a limited amount of time tell, them who you are and what you do. In networking there is two-way communication; you talk then listen. If this is your sole form of income then I estimate you spending at least 2 hours of your day networking. This obviously won't be a continuous amount of time. It would be over a course of time throughout the day. You may think your schedule is too condensed for you to carve out time for networking. Here are some great ways to fit it into your schedule:

- While at the grocery shopping
- Waiting in the coffee shop
- Mingling at church
- Introducing yourself at community events
- Attending networking mixers
- Paying for space at vendor showcases
- While at your or your child's school
- Casual mentions while in the office break room
- Small talk with a stranger while getting your car serviced
- Talking to someone while waiting in the doctor's office
- When you see an old classmate from high school

As you can see anytime is a great time to network. You will definitely have to step outside of your comfort zone. There is no shyness in business. A strong confidence level will help you with this. Being organized and having a high-certainty in your products will also give you a big confidence boost. My recommendation is to always look like your craft, look entrepreneurial. Dress your best and for the part you are claiming to be. Power suits are perfect for big events when you know you will be presenting to a crowd or key investors. I highly suggest joining a professional organization or local chapter in your field (i.e. American Medical Association, Society of Professional Accountants). This will allow you to mingle with like-minded people that you could also feed off of. You pick their brain and likewise, they pick your brain. It will make your more comfortable to be surrounded and learn from peers, so when you are faced a networking opportunity you will be ready.

Please understand every opportunity to connect is not a good one. Unfortunately, you aren't exempt to the woes of linking with the wrong person. I feel it a part of the trial and error process that every entrepreneur goes through. You will need to put some of the practices we mentioned previously in the book into play. Remember, you can't tell everything you know. Some things are specific secrets of your business's success. Is that something you really want to share in networking? Be mindful of those who want to be in your shoes. They will poke, prod and ask many questions and it's ok. Engage in conversation that will result in a sale.

"The difference between ordinary and extraordinary is~ EXTRA! If you want to be extraordinary you have to be willing to do extra."

Pastor Robert Sampson

Full Deliverance Ministries

Summerville, SC

CHAPTER EIGHT

Time Management

"A just weight and balance are the Lord's: all the weights of the bag are his work."
- Proverbs 16:11 (KJV)

It may take you a month or even a year to launch your business. There is no set time frame, so this will be different for every start-up business. God requires some things of you during this time as you prepare to present your business to the public. My first advice to you is to make sure that you are mentally ready to do this. Although this may constantly be on your mind, this can be your constant focus. You must give your brain some downtime. A burned out body, is just like a burned out electrical socket, if you add too much voltage, it will surge in a negative way which could lead to self-destruction. Don't let your passion become an obsession. Just like if you work(ed) a 9-to-5 job, allow yourself at least 2 days out of the week to focus on maintaining healthy relationships with family, and taking care of yourself.

Make sure your mind is free of outside distractions. You cannot do your best work when you are pressured and pressed for time. That is the most important lesson you can learn from time management. Your pace will be the determining factor in whether you produce a good product/service or a great product/service. Personally, I could not write this chapter without having lived through the good and the bad of time management. Managing my time was not my strong suit; however I found truth and help in the scripture selected as the foundation of this chapter.

Let's think about an old weight scale for a moment. If something is heavier than one side, then one side is leaning lower than the other. If both sides are of equal weight then the scale is balanced. It is also like this with our lives if we don't prioritize our time appropriately. Looking at the twenty-four hours in a day, how much time do you think you should dedicate to your new venture daily to bring it to full fruition? Well, if God asks for 10% of our time I think it's safe to say that we can also dedicate 10% of our time to a vision that God has birthed through you. After all, in the end your success is a testament to all who are able to witness it.

To better manage my time, I make a daily schedule for myself. I carve out a set time for specific tasks and create a "to do" list, so I know exactly what my upcoming days look like. We have to take accountability for ourselves and be willing to go whenever duty calls. You are not allowed to have bad days. Even when I encounter a crisis, I tell myself that I must stay on task; you must do the same. For example, if a loved one is hospitalized, we have to make a decision. I have found that staying busy and productive takes my mind off of my crisis. How will you remain busy and productive when a crisis arises? You have a priority to perform business duties that you are locked into. Your level of commitment must align with your business.

Anyone who works in a customer service, should focus on providing good customer service. So, any attitude that you deliver to your customers is going to be delivered back to you. If you provide poor service, you may receive poor pay or no pay at all. Don't let life get in the way of how you make your living and never let them see you sweat!

"Plan your work and work your plan."

Rev. Oddie Smalls

Healing Hurts

Ridgeville, SC

CHAPTER NINE

Operations

"Work hard and become a leader; be lazy and never succeed."
- Proverbs 12:24 (TLB)

Business operations typically involve your day to day processes used to provide the highest quality goods and/or services the company provides. If you've followed all of the steps in the book, but lack in precise and consistent business operations, you will face trials. Here are a few terms that will help you in your journey to becoming a great manager and an excellent leader that produces results:

Management

Believe it or not a good leader could be a horrible manager and a great manager could be a horrible leader. Although we use the terms interchangeably at times there is a huge difference, and both are necessary to have a balance in command. Managers are more responsible for the outcomes and overseeing the day to day operations. They are looking for a control; a group that can produce based on the company's requirements. They will be more focused on the number of bodies available to get the job done and the ratio of time necessary to complete the tasks. Managers also will be more involved with the budget; especially over their own department within a business. Small business owners play dual roles when they are the only ones.

Management Styles

There may be times in the business setting that you may possess one or all of these management styles. It will certainly depend on the task at hand. Take into consideration these styles when dealing with various jobs and the various types of employees that will be performing the jobs. Remember as a manager your biggest responsibility is overseeing the project until its completion. You are responsible for the outcome.

- o **Directive** – dispatch orders and have high

standards; disciplining employees when standards aren't met

- **Authoritative** – they are visionaries who will give their vision to the team and expect the employees to make it come to light

- **Affiliative** – this type of leader likes to bond with their employees and can sometimes become a nuisance if the bonding is preventing the staff from working.

- **Participative** – is democratic in style and will often give employees the option to vote to help make decisions as it pertains to the business

- **Pacesetting** – they set the pace of the workflow from the beginning; their management style results in a very productive team who has high energy, team engagement and are highly motivated

- **Coaching** – the coach focuses on the learning experience and how well the team absorbed and applied the information to the daily tasks

Leadership

Leadership has more direct involvement with the staff. A Leader can be described as a coach or motivator ensuring the staff has everything they need to get their job done.

The sociology of knowing and understanding who works for you will help you understand how to handle situations. While disciplinary actions will be in place for all, generations have a different psyche when it comes to the definition of work versus job versus career. Some people are natural born leaders and others are trained in the skill of leading. In essence it is all about relationships and how well you understand the needs of others who are connected to you.

To truly understand this theory, let's reference a great psychologist, Abraham Maslow. In 1943 he developed a pyramid that explained how people are motivated called, Maslow's Hierarchy of Needs, pictured below:

SCRIPTURALLY STRUCTURED

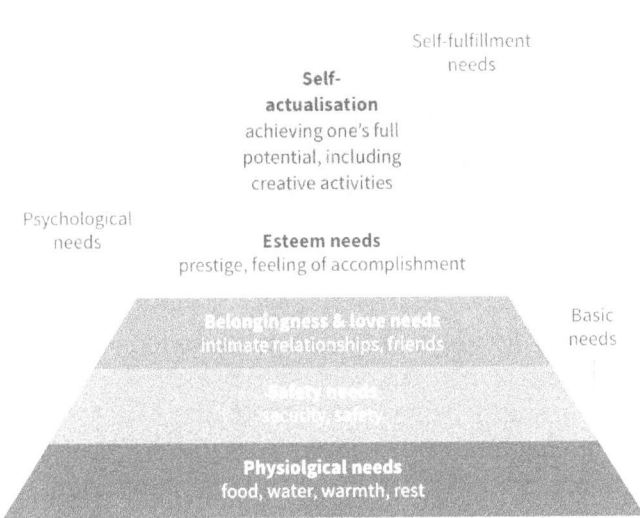

This pyramid, read from bottom to top, lists our needs from the most basic necessities of our basic everyday needs which are food, water, rest and warmth. As a manager or leader in the workplace this is a need you cannot supply directly, but compensation your staff will allow them to provide this for themselves. The next is safety needs; in the workplace you are responsible for the safety of your employees, whether they are in your comfortable office or they are on a dangerous construction site. The next set of needs is psychological and although you may not think so, these needs too, can be met in the workplace. Allowing someone to feel like they belong or are liked by the manager and staff is important and can determine how a person performs. If they are performing below standard, it may be because they have low self-esteem and are feeling unaccomplished. Giving them more responsibilities or allowing them to learn something new once they have accomplished one goal will help them reach their highest potential and in essence will take them to their highest point in realizing who they are and where they fit in your company and in society. That would be the point of self-actualization. This process could take longer for some and sometimes causes a riff in the relationship scheme of the workplace. Don't worry, there are other ways to help. Along someone's journey in a new career/job/role, it is important to reward them. There are two types of rewards:

- **Tangible Rewards** - Things that a person can physically see or touch, for example a bonus, overtime, a certificate or something they can display.

- **Intangible rewards** – Telling them they are doing a good job or acknowledging their great works in a staff meeting or via social media

Leadership Styles

It is very important to learn and become familiar with the different types of leadership styles. You must also determine if your leadership style matches your type of business, employees and customers. What type of leader are you?

- **Laissez-Faire** - A laissez-faire leader lacks direct supervision of employees and fails to provide regular feedback to those under his supervision

- **Autocratic** - The autocratic leadership style allows managers to make decisions alone without the input of others

- **Participative** - Participative leadership boosts employee morale because employees make contributions to the decision-making process

- **Transactional -** Managers and team members set predetermined goals together, and employees agree to follow the direction and leadership of the manager to accomplish those goals

- **Transformational -** Leaders motivate employees and enhance productivity and efficiency through communication and high visibility

Types of Employees

It is as equally important to learn and become familiar with the different types of employees. Learning your employees will help you to better communicate with and understand them. What type(s) of employees do you have?

- **Centennials: Born 1996 and later** - In 2006 there were a record number of births in the US and 49% of those born were Hispanic, this will change the American melting pot in terms of behavior and culture. The number of births in 2006 far outnumbered the start of the baby boom generation, and they will easily be a larger generation.

- **Millennials: Born 1977 to 1995** - Prefer digital literacy as they grew up in a digital environment. Have never known a world without computers! They get all their information and most of their socialization from the Internet.

- **Generation X: Born 1965 to 1976** - Tend to commit to self rather than an organization or specific career. This generation averages 7 career changes in their lifetime, it was not normal to work for a company for life, unlike previous generations.

- **Baby Boomers: Born 1946 to 1964** - Tend to be more positive about authority, hierarchal structure and tradition.

- **Traditionalists: Born 1945 and before** - There was no "retirement." You worked until you died or couldn't work anymore.

Most entrepreneurs are Generation X. I myself fall into that category and after studying this information I can say that I understand me a little bit better. Consider this information when you are assigning specific job duties to employees in your business. Also, consider this when you are conducting business as an entrepreneur looking to secure new contracts. A baby boomer or traditionalist may not patron someone whose work ethic they cannot respect. Don't allow these characteristics to prevent you from securing new business.

Worksite

Think about your current or future worksite/ workspace. Become familiar with your space and put plans in place to make sure it is suited to serve your initial business needs. Also, think about your goals and the length of time that you plan to remain in your initial worksite/workspace before growing into something new.

- Working remotely from home?
- Do you have a retail office space?
- Will your employees have to travel from various worksites?
- Will they work from a church or educational organization?

Equipment

Does your business venture need equipment? Think about the kinds of equipment you will need to get started initially. Do some research to get the best deal on needed equipment for your start-up. It is wise to find used or refurbished equipment and supplies. Will your business require the following?

- o Company vehicle
- o Computers
- o Machinery

Day to Day Operations

Picture your day-to-day operations. Establish a schedule that will benefit your customers and clients. Remember there should be a set base schedule. However, your schedule and operations should be expandable to meet the needs of your current clients and to grow to meet the needs of your future clients. Keep the answers to the following questions in mind:

- o How many individuals does it take to accomplish the task at hand?
- o What are some things a business and its employees will engage in on a daily basis

for the purposes of generating a profit and increasing the inherent value of the business?

Although the chapter is entitled business operations; I've provided you with a wealth of information on leadership and management styles. The fact is this is what will make your business successful. You have to know how to lead in order to for others to want to follow you. By understanding all of the principles given you will be able to efficiently operate your business.

"Don't expect the same results starting out as someone else who's been in business for years. Stay focused on your mission and pace yourself. You cannot do it all in one day."

Pastor Eddrena M. Goodwin

Kingdom Revelation Worship Center

Summerville, SC

CHAPTER TEN

Conclusion

"There is no wisdom, no insight, no plan
that can succeed against the Lord."
- Proverbs 21:30 (NIV)

"And God is able to bless you abundantly, so
that in all things at all times, having all that you
need, you will abound in every good work.
- 2 Corinthians 9:8 (NIV)

Whether new or established it doesn't hurt to be reminded of some of these helpful tips to help you not lose sight of the lessons in the scripture. This book is everything I wish I had when I started my first business. No matter what type of business you have, these same concepts will apply. Make no mistake, God keeps his promises. We've provided you with two scriptures one from the Old Testament which conceals the scripture and one from the New Testament which reveals the scripture message. God will bless you and your business plentifully.

Your hard work is far from over. I used Proverbs 21:30 to remind you that in business sometimes competitors don't play fair, sometimes we make bad decisions and sometimes things just will not go your way. It just means it's time to seek God for a new plan, new insight and new wisdom. Fear not, even during difficult times you can rest assured that your answer will lie in the scriptures of the Holy Bible.

The final phase of any business is measuring its success. How would you rate your business now that you are an accomplished entrepreneur? Start by looking at your finances to see if your revenue is higher than your expenses and other liabilities. It's not always the dollars that tell you if you are successful or not. You should also survey your customers to determine how many are new versus your loyal patrons. Look at how they rate your service and if there are any areas you can improve. If you are losing customers or you have a particular product or service that is not working out well; how can you make it better? Does your own rating compared to your customer's rating meet your approval? Next measure your growth; again, if there is none work on it. Find a new consumer base, network, and utilize local media outlets.

Congratulations! Your business is now Scripturally Structured and a step above the rest.

ABOUT THE AUTHOR

Jennifer S. Simmons, a South Carolina native, is a career-driven individual. With an undergraduate degree in Business Management and a Master's Degree in Business Administration; she learned at an early age the secret to success is hard work coupled with strong faith. In 2009, Jennifer began a journey with gospel recording artist Natasha Gray and Grammy-nominated producer Rodrick Cliche with the assigned role of Executive Business Manager of Jeneyus Productions. Through this experience came the birth of Music Media Management; a company who serves as an advocate for those in the entertainment industry.

Music continues to be a driving force in her life as she undertakes several roles. More recently she has served as the Marketing Manager for an independent film entitled, "Escaped To Tell". She is also the host and founder of "The Je` Shennel and Keymiel Show", a radio show focused on educating and promoting independent Christian artists.

Giving back to the community is extremely important to her. Ms. Simmons is a mentor in her community and also provides free tutoring, resume writing classes and career counseling assistance.

She is set to launch her newest endeavor, Certitude Health Coding Educators in April of 2017. As a career certified medical coder and licensed instructor, she is looking forward to helping individuals become gainfully employed in the progressive field of healthcare.

www.ingramcontent.com/pod-product-compliance
Lightning Source LLC
Chambersburg PA
CBHW071823200526
45169CB00018B/988